Memories of

This updated booklet covers the areas of P
written on earlier and brings the story forward to the sixties.

The area we now know as Portsea lies on what was once part of one of the common fields of the town of Portsmouth, now Old Portsmouth. Fountain Field as it was originally called reached from the shore on the west to the Mill Pond on the east and as far north as Kingston Crescent. The field was gradually split up into smaller units and in 1495 the Dockyard was built on part of it. The Mill Pond was a tidal inlet which reached up to Lake Road and despite being slowly reclaimed had a seamill until 1868 which must have looked similar to the one at Emsworth. The only other early buildings on the common were Beeston's great barn, a wheelwrights and a smithy. There were also several rows of trees sheltering ropewalks.

When William Shakespear built the old gunwharf in 1662 he extracted soil from the common to reclaim land from the sea and later gravel was extracted from the common leaving several large pits. One stretched from Bonfire Corner to Kent Street and Queen Street crossed it by a bridge, Battle Bridge. Another large pit was between St. James's Street and Bishop Street.

In the late seventeenth century, to avoid the long detour around the Mill Pond, Dockyard workers started erecting houses on the common but the Governor of Portsmouth threatened to fire his guns at them. When Queen Anne and her husband, Prince George of Denmark, visited Portsmouth the shipwrights made a deputation to them and on the Prince's intervention the Governor relented. As the common had originally been under cultivation by means of strips, when the plots were sold it meant that streets were narrow and houses small. By 1716 many of the main streets had been laid out. In 1736, William Edge settled the gravel pits and other land on his daughter, the wife of George Shakespear of London, who laid out the streets between Hanover Street and St James Street.

In the late eighteenth century court and alley tenements were built in the grounds of the previous houses. These were one up and one down back to back dwellings which allowed many families to live in a very small area and later caused the slum problems of the area. At about the same time larger building plots were becoming available and large fine houses were built in the St George's Square area.

"As a child in 1934 my brothers and I would be taken on a Sunday evening down Queen Street to the Hard by our Mum and Dad together with her brother, Arch Clarke, and his wife, Auntie Alice, their young son Billie, walking all the way from Crasswell Street, Landport to the Hard. When we entered Queens Street from Edinburgh Road the scene changed - we had entered the most notorious ward of the Town, Portsea.

Portsea was well known for its impoverished inhabitants, slums, prostitution, crime. My uncle Arch was a Chief Petty Officer, and when he was on leave, he and our parents would enjoy walking through this crowded thoroughfare with all its shops, the pavements crowded with sailors in their smart naval uniforms. As children we were fascinated by the displays in the windows of the shops for even on Sunday with all of them closed you would see a variety of goods that you would not find in such a small area any where in the town. This was the main shopping area for the hundreds of sailors that were in the Naval Barracks and the crews of ships in the Dockyard and harbour plus the thousands of inhabitants of the surrounding slums, the most densely populated ward in the town.

When we eventually arrived at the Hard we would be taken to the children's room in one of the numerous pubs, given crisps or a packet of cheese biscuits with a glass of lemonade whilst our parents enjoyed their beer and a chat. After a stay of an hour or so we would walk back to Landport on a fine evening having enjoyed a most enjoyable outing arriving home tired and ready for bed.

As we grew older whilst we were on holiday from school we, would venture down to this place of interest where, we would have interesting adventures, watching the fishermen boiling the tar and then painting their boats with it while it was still boiling after repairing them, playing on huge logs that were tethered with iron chains, there to season in the sea. We would run across these logs especially when the tide was up and they were afloat and moving with the motion of the sea. If the tide was out we would go under the Harbour railway via the logs and watch the men playing pitch and toss and gambling - a dangerous pastime for if they were caught they would be heavily fined and punished.

When I was older and in the eleven plus group at Arundel Street School, one day a week we were sent to Kent Street School to be taught basic working skills in woodwork and metalwork. To get there I and my class mates would have to walk through Queen Street and at eight-thirty in the morning it seethed with activities. The shops were open and the pavements crowded, for the day started early in this narrow thoroughfare where the locals knew that only those who shopped early got the best bargains. My mate and I would linger by the Naval Barracks gates, for every morning at the time we were passing the Naval Band marched out led by their magnificent Drum Major who would toss his staff as they came through the barrack gate archway and catch it on the other side. Everyday they marched a working party of sailors down to the dockyard and to us youngsters a thrilling stirring sight, but the street was always busy and unlike now every other person being a sailor resplendent in uniform, but to us school children there was always the danger we would linger too long looking in the shop windows. For there were dozens of shop windows which appealed to the sense of adventure in we boys, by their displays of life in the Navy but our time keeping was regulated by the knowledge we would receive a stroke of the masters cane across the palm of your hand a very painful experience!

There were no unruly classes in Kent Street Manual. In fact some of the boys would play truant rather than suffer this harsh discipline, but once I got used to the work it was interesting and you were taught the basic skills of woodwork and metalwork which made it all worth while. Some of the items you made you were allowed to take home, which was an encouragement to acquire and improve your ability in these skills you were taught despite the severity of the teaching staff's techniques, which on reflection were very necessary where they had classes of at least forty boys who were working with sharp tools.

Later, after I had met my wife to be, I was told by her mum that she had worked in Cavender's cigarette and snuff factory in what was then the Queens Cinema and the working conditions in which she had endured there.

My fiancee, Miss Phyllis Chase, was the manageress of Timothy Whites hardware store on the corner of North Street. In 1941 when we first began our association it was a thriving business. What was more amazing was the relationship of the shop keepers to one another. They looked after each other's interests and often Phyllis would have the opportunity to buy a pair of wild rabbits from the butcher, Mr Hutchins, a blessing in the time when rationing was severe. Others would give her the opportunity to buy goods that were in short supply, but in 1941 this was one of the most dangerous areas in the city because of it being so close to the Dockyard and Naval Barracks.

I well remember going through Queens Street at night after a raid to pick up unfortunate casualties, seeing the windows of shops and public houses blown out with people still drinking among the debris in the pubs. To myself proof of the courage in this the poorest and most deprived part of the City.

Another time I was asked to go to Lion Terrace after it had been bombed to pick up body parts that had been found during rescue work. It was mid morning with the local people walking by taking the debris and turmoil as something they accepted as normal. I never failed to be impressed by the fact that they stayed in the area knowing how dangerous it was and the risks they suffered in staying. Of course most of them being Dockyard employees they could not afford the expense of being too far from their place of employment or accommodation outside of the town, for the Dockyard in time of war was working to its full capacity repairing and servicing the Navy and needed all the skills the work force possessed in carrying out this responsibility.

One afternoon I received a phone call whilst at work from Phyllis' shop telling me that whilst she had been cycling to work she had been involved in an accident with a Naval lorry. I spoke to my foreman who sent me down to Touts in Queens Street supposedly to pick up material to repair a truck. In reality, so I could find out what had happened and do what I could to help. When I arrived she was sitting on a chair bruised all down her right side, could not walk and very distressed. It appeared the driver of the lorry had stopped and not troubled to give her his details but saying take this pound for its seems your stockings are spoilt and then went on his way! I loaded her and her bike into the van and took them home. Nothing more was done in the matter but it took weeks for the injury to remedy itself. She was a victim of the war and compared to what happened to others during the Air Raids was a minor event.

One of my lasting happy memories of the street was being invited to tea with Mr and Mrs Morris the watchmender and jeweller next to Timothy Whites. The occasion being that Phyllis told them of our marriage arrangements, a gesture that was typical of the friendly people of Queen Street."

Frank Deacon

Much of the area was affected by bomb damage in the Second World War and in 1957 more properties were demolished and replaced by flats in the 1957 slum clearance programme. Where contributors to our earlier books gave details of the housing conditions in the early years we have included those to show what the area was like before the clearance programmes.

Many of the streets in Portsea number differently from other roads in Portsmouth, instead of odd numbers and even numbers they are numbered consecutively on one side returning on the other side. The following listing is based on the 1960 Kellys trade directory.

Admiralty Road, known as Chapel Row until 1902.
7 Brickwoods Limited, The Portsmouth Brewery

Brewery Offices in Chapel Road

The earliest part of the site was the Catherine Brewery, which was moved here from Sandwich Street in 1845 by John Methuin when the Sandwich Street area was absorbed into the Dockyard. The brewery was used by the Methuin family and their tenants until December 1848 when Dormer Jewell purchased the brewery for £650. The brewery expanded under the ownership of the Jewells with its own wells, one 750 feet deep, the other 615 feet deep and by 1899 they had seventy tied houses. The next change of owner came in 1899 when the family that became most famous as Portsmouth brewers bought the premises, starting with John & Arthur Brickwood. They expanded and rebuilt the brewery in 1903 and in 1911 renamed the brewery the Portsmouth Brewery taking the name from the Pike Spicer brewery in Old Portsmouth that they had recently bought. As late as 1962 another expansion,took place and in 1969 the premises on the other side of Cross Street were erected as a wine and spirit store. The brewery came under control of Whitbread and in 1983 the last brew was made on the site. The bottling plant and storehouse buildings were sold to Allders Department store for use as a warehouse whilst the brewery and plant was demolished to form the Heritage Car Park. All that remained in 2005 were the office buildings on the Admiralty Road frontage which were demolished in 2006 for the Admiralty Quarter development.

8 Sunshine Hotels Ltd

Old house on corner of Aylward Street and Kent Street

Aylward Street

The house pictured was demolished in 2007.

East Side

Jacob's Terrace

West Side

13 George Cash & Co. Ltd., Brass Founders
13 Robert Wood & Son Ltd., Brass Finishers
The foundry and other buildings were demolished in 1976 and Foundry Court flats built on the site by the James Butcher Housing Association.

"In 1939 we moved to a flat in Aylward Street. A top floor flat in a three storey high block, it was more comfortable than our house in Hilsea and nearer our work. With the half a crown I got for pocket money, I could go to the Queen's Picture House and buy a bag of chips on my night out. In the clothes drying area between the flats we used to play football with a tennis ball. There must have been about fifty of us chasing the ball, the only way I could see the ball was by being the goalkeeper. The elderly people in the bottom flats were up in arms because of the noise and danger to their windows.

A brick air-raid shelter was built between the blocks. We used to go around to put our incendiaries, then one night the siren went off and mum got us all into the shelter. Then she told me to go back and turn the lights out but when I went to into the kitchen I found an incendiary under the clothes mangle. There was a tea chest used a a dirty washing basket standing in the kitchen and that was on fire. I put that out with a few bowls of water. There was a hole in the ceiling over the draining board, I threw a few bowls of water over the bomb but it would not go out so I got a bucket and went down to get some soil. When Mum asked me why I had not put out the light I told her there was a bomb there. She and Dad were up the stairs in a rush, when I got back, there was an Air Raid Warden lying on the floor spraying the bomb with water from a stirrup pump. My bit of dirt wasn't wanted. The next day there was a write up about it in the Evening News with a photo of Dorrie standing on a chair pointing to the hole. That was just one bit of excitement, from then on we spent many a night running around putting out incendiaries. I was given a job at the Malthouse in St Georges Square, not far from where we lived. When I got there I found that a bomb had blown up the stables and there were four or five shire horses lying dead. The Malthouse was in working order so we were given the job of turning the malt mill until we were wanted back at the brewery. We were given various jobs till the new fridges were fixed up then I was caught skylarking. I was then sent to the scalding yard where I had to stack and scrub dirty barrels. I soon got used to that work and the barrels got lighter as I got stronger. The part I did not like was the drips of water, dripping down my neck. I had to wear wooden clogs with steel soles and heels, I had to learn to walk in them. I think they ruined my feet forever."

Ron Bradshaw.

Beck Street, named after Maurice Beck, auctioneer who died in 1877. The street was known from 1774 as Pud's Lane and was presumably re-named shortly after the death of Mr Beck.

North Side

E.A.G., Scrap Metal

Bishop Street, many properties were demolished in the 1957 slum clearance programme.

East Side

W. Treadgold & Co. Ltd., Iron Merchants
Lestock House, named after Admiral Lestock, demolished by 2004.
Barham House, named after Admiral Barham, demolished by 2004.
Modern terraced housing now occupies the site of the two blocks of flats.

West Side

W. Treadgold & Co. Ltd., Iron, Steel & Sheet Metal Merchants

Founded by William Treadgold in 1847. The business survived until 1988 when it closed. The whole of the premises and stock were sold to Hampshire County Council and the building converted into a museum, opening in 1995. It is currently closed.

Rooke House, named after Admiral Rooke.
Kempenfelt House, named after Admiral Kempenfelt

Blossom Alley

Used to run from Cross Street to North Street. The houses in the alley and courts off of it were demolished in 1929 when the medical officer of health condemned the 17 houses in the alley.

In 1923 the alley was the scene of a murder. Mary Pelham, 38, who lived at number 14 was found on Saturday 23rd of January having been hit over the head with a bottle and then strangled in her bed. Born in Leeds she became a domestic servant, married Henry Pelham and moved to Brighton when her husband left to fight in the First World War. She moved to Portsmouth in 1918 to sell flowers by day and herself at night and was known as Brighton Mary. On his return and finding out what his wife was up to he left her. It was thought that a sailor from the nearby barracks was the murderer as the scarf with which she was strangled was tied in a Naval knot.

Although called an alley it still had other courts leading off of it, one was Witley Place.

"I lived in Witley Place in 1921 with my wife and three children, there were ten dwellings. They had two rooms, one up, one down. The rent was 7/-, (35p) a week. There was a water tap and toilet outside."

Mr William Ponsford 1975

Britain Street

"41 Britain Street in the 1920s was a very old house with a bay window. There was a basement but it was never used, as it was blocked off for some reason. On the ground floor was a small sitting room, where the family did their cooking. Two families shared the outside toilet and wash-house. Above the sitting room was one bedroom and above that was another but this could not be used as the roof was dangerous. The rent was 6/-, (30p), a week."

Mrs Alice Rowsell 1975

Leading off from Britain Street was Taylors Court, that dated from at least 1848.

"I lived at 7 Taylors Court in the 1920s. The rent was around 4/6, (22.5p). The house had a room and kitchen downstairs and two rooms upstairs and an attic. There was a water tap outside and a flush toilet and wash-house used by all the tenants. Meals were cooked on a fire in the ground floor room, in later years a gas cooker was introduced. The houses were very old. There were cupboards in the living room and kitchen for brooms, food, crocks and coal. Mrs Valerio was the landlady. She made the tenants scrub the fronts of their houses each morning. The tenants took it in turn to clean out the W.C. and wash-house. The rubbish and dirt was thrown into a large bin at the back of the wash-house and this was collected by the corporation each week."

Mrs F Bowbrick 1975

"I used to live at 8 Taylors Court. The rent was 5/-, (25p), a week. There were fourteen houses in the Court. In each dwelling there was a living room and back room on the ground floor. Cooking was done on a range in the backroom. There were two bedrooms upstairs and an attic above them. There was a tap in the alleyway for all the houses in the court. A wash house and lavatory were also shared. The landlord was Mr Valerio, who was an ice-cream manufacturer (He is listed in the Kellys at 37 Britain Street)."

Mrs Emma Smallbones 1975

East Side

Alfred Stocker, beer retailer
Fraser House, named after Dr Mearns Fraser who ordered the slum clearance.
Besant House, named after Walter Besant, local author.
These new flats were built in 1953 by local builder John Lay.

Butcher Street

East Side

16	M.Wales, Fried fish shop
17-19	C.Warn, Grocer
24	Cole Bros (W.Cole), Butchers

West Side

29	C.Warn, Bakery
35-37	S.E.B. Upholstery(Portsmouth) Ltd, Manufacturing Upholsterers. Warehouse.
	Founded by Henry Buxton in 1896, the company was formed by

his son Sidney E Buxton. They moved to Western Road, were later taken over by Furniture Land who closed the business.

Clock Street

Residential only.
Formerly since 1773 until 1888 the Vine public house was on the 'east' side. Then it changed name to The Benbow until 1918.

College Lane

No properties

Old shop on corner of Clock Street

College Street
Portsea Branch Post Office

Cross Street

West Side

here are Daniel Street and Bonfire Corner

East Side

here is Cumberland Street
54 Frank Pinhorne, Butcher
56 Charles Ewer, Grocer

here is King Street
56a Shamrock Tavern
Dates back as far as 1716 when it was known as the King's Head. In 1784 it was known as The King's Head & Mitre; returning to just plain King's Head from 1823 until 1863. In 1865 it gains the distinction of King's Head Tavern. By 1874 it was referred to as The Shamrock and is later listed either as Shamrock or Shamrock Tavern until 1962. The number has changed over the years as well, starting at 55, then 56 and sometimes as 29 King Street.

57a Alfred Stallard, Coal Merchant

here is Blossom Alley
57 Donald Thorne, Café

here is Prince George Street

61 Ernest Hull, Boot Repairer
61 London & Southern, Wholesale Grocers
64 Mrr M Ewer, Shopkeeper
66 Harry Laufer, Tailor

56a Cross Street on corner with King Street

Cumberland Street, named after the Duke of Cumberland

South Side

Jenkins House, demolished prior to 1996. Probably named after the City Engineer.
Emanuel House, named after Alderman Emanuel Emanuel, demolished by 2005.
Beresford House, named after Admiral Lord Beresford, demolished by 1996.
Blackthorn Terrace, Pounds Terrace and another terrace of houses now occupy the site of these three blocks of flats.

North Side

Flats 2-24 were renovated and then named Brickwood House
Privett House, named after Councillor F.J.Privett, J.P Renovated and grounds landscaped in recent years.
Cumberland House, as with the street named after the Duke of Cumberland.

Curzon Howe Road, named after Admiral Sir Assheton Curzon-Howe. The road was built in 1911 as part of the slum clearance project for Portsea ordered by Dr Mearns Fraser the medical office for health.
Residential Only

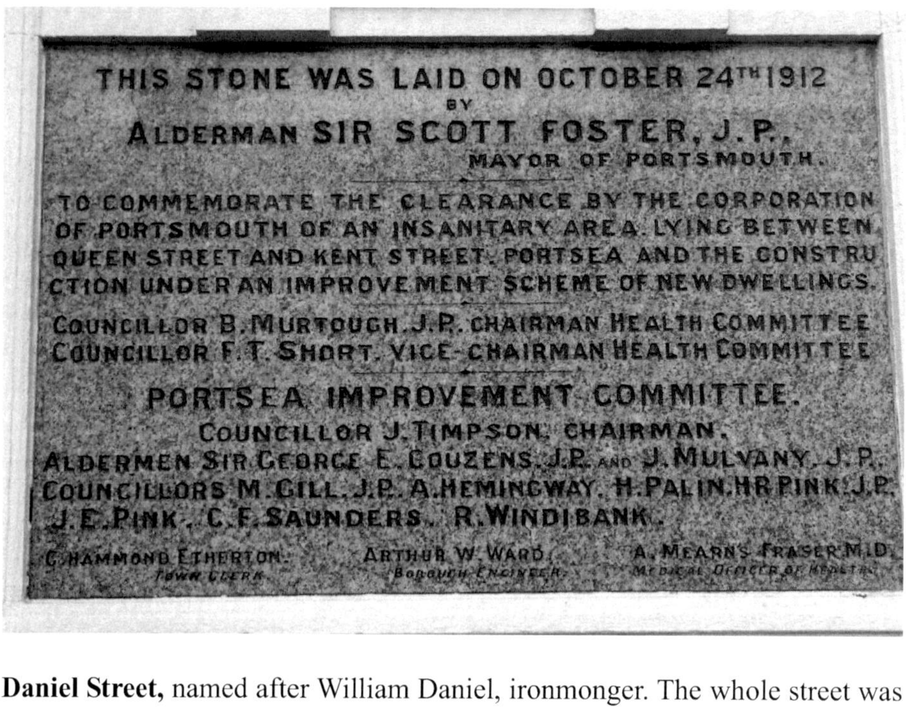

Daniel Street, named after William Daniel, ironmonger. The whole street was absorbed into Brickwoods Brewery.

No properties although the frontage of the former Methodist Church could be seen until the brewery was demolished.

The church was built in 1779 as St Peters Free Anglican. In 1800 it was bought by the Wesleyans. They enlarged the chapel in 1810 and installed gas lighting in 1821. As the brewery surrounded the premises there were several discussions with Brickwoods about them buying the church from the 1880s and finally in 1913 the church was sold and the congregation moved to Queen Street. Brickwoods converted the church into a store.

Hanover Street, named after the Royal Family.
Calder House, named after Admiral Calder.

Hard, real name was Ship and Castle Row, but took its name from the Common Hard - the spit of land out to sea opposite.

East Side

1	Ship & Castle First listed in 1700 and in use until 1975. The building was derelict until 1979. In 1980 the interior was demolished leaving only the outer walls standing. It re-opened in Aug 1981. In Feb 1992 the pub re-opened after refurbishment.
2	Gieves Ltd., Stationers
3-5	Norman Radford, Motor Car Dealer Now Hooper Court flats
6	W. Cooper (Harwich) Outfitters
7	E. E Harris & Co. Ltd., Café. Later became a fish and chip shop which it remains today - The Britannia
9	King & Queen First listed in 1798. The pub was rebuilt in 1924 to designs of local architect A.E.Cogswell.
10	Ship Anson, William Hawkes First listed in 1784 as The New Anson it became the Ship Anson by 1823. In 1906 it was re-fronted to designs of local architect V.G.Cogswell, son of A.E.Cogswell. In recent years the King and Queen pub next door has been incorporated into the building.

Daniel Street, frontage of former Church

11 Jerome Goss, Tobacconist
Now Victory News

12-14 Moss Bros & Co., Outfitters
A modern office block was built in this corner, later refurbished and converted into flats, Warrior House

here is Clock Street

15-16 John Harvey & Son Ltd., Wine & Spirit Merchants
In 1823 was James Stokes, Wine & Spirits, becoming Stokes & Co. by 1863. In 1933 became Stokes & Harvey - the Harvey being Harveys of Bristol. Originally only at number 15.
The premises later became a public house, the Ship Leopard in 1976 replacing the pub of the same name in Havant Street. It closed and in 1990 re-opened as Hard Times, a Dicken's themed house. This closed in 1994 and then re-opened as McCoys named after the pub company run by David Jones. In 2003 David Jones renovated the pub and it reverted back to the name Ship Leopard and was opened by Lord Mayor, Tom Blair, on 1 Jul 2003.

17-18 National Provincial Bank
Note the date stone, 1874 over the door. The upper floors have been converted to flats whilst the Genesis Exhibition occupies the ground floor.

19-20 Car Park for Keppels Head, due to have a six storey block of flats erected on it.
Earlier 19 was the Sheer Hulk from 1823 to 1940 a Bidens of Gosport pub.

21 Saccone & Speed Ltd., Wine & Spirit Merchants
From 1693 until 1918 was the Nag's Head or variations. By 1920 it was Saccone & Speed, off licence. In 1992 it went back to on licence as the Lady Hamilton.

22 Gieves Ltd., Outfitters
The shop was built in 1909 to designs of local architect A.E.Cogswell to replace the shop that had been in the High Street since at least 1785 when Melchizdeck Meredith was the proprietor. The Gieve family connection started in 1852. Although bombed in 1941 the shop was restored and traded here until they moved to the new

development at Gunwharf Quays. The premises have since been refitted and is currently a Portsea Co-operative Store with flats above.

24-26 Keppel's Hotel Ltd, N.W.McCaw & Mrs McCaw
The Keppel's Head here since 1784 named after Admiral Augustus Keppel. Many pubs were named after the Admiral when he was acquitted at court martial in 1779. It burnt down on 25 April 1803 but the owner Mr Wickenden and his servants were saved. A public subscription was raised as Mr Wickenden was uninsured and £400 raised. It has been rebuilt several times expanding to take in neighbouring properties on the Hard.

27 Gillot & Hasell, Naval Outfitters - see the parapet where the name remains

28 S.W.Silver & Co., Outfitters
Later was a Wimpy Bar Café before becoming a Chinese Take-Way.

here are College Street and College Lane

33-34 Lloyds Bank Ltd, now a taxi office.
Brunel House a large office block for the Inland Revenue and Dept of Environment was built here but has stood empty for many years.

West Side

George Warren, Fruiterer
D.A.Reddish, Café
Cabmen's & Watermen's Shelter
Portsmouth Harbour Pier
Originally built as the Royal Albert Pier (Portsea Pier), it opened on 1st Jun 1847. It was 1249 feet long and cost £1,200. It later became the Harbour Station.
Port of Portsmouth Steam Launch & Towing Co. Ltd., Gosport Ferry

Havant Street, earlier known as Head and Horn Row. Some properties were demolished in 1957 slum clearance program, while nearby new flats were being built.

North Side

25	William Edmunds, Newsagent
26	Ship Leopard, Alfred Pinches Listed in trade directories as early as 1784 when it was the Leopard, by 1823 the name changed to Ship Leopard. In 1968 a CPO was issued and the pub closed in 1971.
27-29	City Garages (Portsmouth) Ltd., Motor Engineers
31	J.Starkey & Ltd., cap manufacturers

South Side

In 1969 a large 17 storey office block, Victory House, was built here for the Zurich Insurance Company at a cost of £1m pounds. Zurich moved to Stanhope Road and Pall Europe now occupy the offices.

"I started work for Zurich Insurance on 2nd of April 1970. The building was officially opened by Fritz Gerber and the Lord Mayor W.Evans of Portsmouth on 23rd of April. When I started there was only one building standing opposite the Zurich building which was the original Ship Leopard pub. A lot of staff drank there, but the pub was soon demolished and our usual hostelry was then the Keppels Head. On one occasion I ordered a half pint of lager, this arrived, I picked up the glass and the bottom fell out of it all over my lap and the other female present. A relative of mine worked for Coopers of Harwich at 49 Queens Street for many years, when I needed some yeast for cooking he suggested I try the brewery, Whitbreads. I went over and as well as the yeast I got an invitation to organise a tour of the brewery which I did. Coopers was actually part of C.H.Bernard, although run separately. Mr Cooper had retired to Valetta some years before. Coopers sent vans into the Dockyard to obtain trade, sailors had allotments, monies accrued to buy goods. They produced a catalogue every season. We got good staff discount if we saw anything we wanted, plus a Naval diary every year, this always contained the places named in the shipping forecasts, and lots of diagrams of ships. I looked around the shop just before Coopers moved. There was an area with a cobbled floor and the Queen Ann loft was still and is still there! My relative liked the beat bobby who was Gladys Howard, who later became a City Councillor and Lord Mayor.

When I worked at Zurich, Campions the bakers were still in St Georges Square. I used to park the car at the road side, nothing posh, a yellow Morris 1100. I always washed my car when it was raining copying the staff at the Ambulance Station who hosed the ambulances when it was raining.

At the time I worked for Zurich, there was a four day week and power cuts. The staff had to contemplate walking up and down the stairs instead of using the list. I worked on the 16th floor at the time, but luckily I was in good health. I never remember walking upstairs much but do remember walking down.

There was a paper shortage and we were encouraged to write on the back of paper and to use Snowpak and Tippex, I remember later someone had a tee-shirt with the slogan 'Cover you Boobs with Snowpak'.

Being a highrise and built in the sixties the building was prone to water penetration through the bottom of the windows after deluges, and we would come ion to work and find the maintenance team mopping up the water, at this time we had lino tiles as floor covering so it was relatively easy to deal with.

Battleships were continually passing and so a lot of the previously London based personnel had binoculars. One of the jokers said that he had inadvertently aimed them at the nearby high rise flats - where he observed people didn't bother much with drawing curtains! "

Sylvia Webb

Hawke Street

East Side

Codrington House, named after Admiral Sir Edward Codrington.
Cradock House, named after the Admiral.

West Side

Benbow House, named after the Admiral.
Frobisher House, named after the Admiral.

Hay Street

"In the 1920s Number 12 was made entirely of wood, the only brickwork was the fireplace. The family were very fire conscious and father often used to practice fire drill. Ropes were kept coiled in bedroom cupboards and the children knew how to tie one end to the bed legs and throw the rest out of the windows. The home was a two storey building."

Mrs G Jones 1975

East Side

	J Dagastino (Portsmouth) Ltd., Ice Cream Factory
15	A Fleming & Co.(Outfitters) Ltd., Naval Outfitters

West Side

20	Saxton Metal Co, Metal Merchants
Perkins House	

Kent Street, earlier the Old Rope Walk, 1751 to 1835. Probably named after the Kent family who were farmers on the island and involved in local politics. Some properties were demolished in the 1957 slum clearance programme.

"As a young girl, my mother, two brothers and me went to live with my grandmother who lived in Ranwell's Court. It was a small house of three rooms and a cellar, and one of a group of three. Outside was a small area of grassland, and a big walled pit into which all the rubbish could be thrown. There was only one toilet to share among these three houses and only one water tap, both standing outside in the yard. It meant I had to go outside to wash in all weathers and I was frequently frightened when in the toilet, with the men banging on the door and shouting at me.

The houses backed on to the back of Kent Street Baptist Church. There was a ledge along the wall and my brothers sat me on it and left me there, I kept on crying and calling out, but, had to wait until a man came and got me down. I can remember when a man kept a monkey in Meeting House Alley. This monkey got away and went into the house belonging to the mineral water firm of Murtoughs. The monkey must have run through the house and he suddenly appeared at a bedroom window. He sat on the window sill and had obtained a pipe from somewhere which he was pretending to smoke.

These were hard times and many times I was very hungry. Some mornings I would sit on the steps of one of the houses waiting for people to finish breakfast, then they would come out and offer me the crusts. I can also remember a

Beneficial Society's Primary School, Infants

warehouse which had a rubbish pit at the side, and I used to go there and look for pecked fruit. Saturday morning I used to go with my brothers along the foreshore collecting pieces of wood to store for the fire."

South Side

Campions (Bakers) Ltd
Corporation Flats
61 Leonard Tee, Grocer
63 Thomas Drew & Son, Butchers
Portsea Modern School for Boys, Annexe
Navy, Army & Air Force Institute, Garage

North Side

here are Union & Hanover Streets
G.H.Kirby, Coal Merchants

here is Southampton Row

The Society was established in 1755 as the plaque in the pediment of the building of 1784 states. The building was enlarged to take girls as well as boys in 1836. The society was wound up in 1936.

The building fell into disrepair until 1979 when the City Council bought it and spent £90,000 renovating the building. It is currently boarded up. In Southampton Row is the foundation stone laid by Mayor Edward Carter.

here is Curzon Howe Road

Crown Listed as the Butcher's Arms from 1719 until 1956, then the Crown from 1958 until 1978. Then from 1992 until 2002 when it was demolished known as the Portsea Arms.

here is Bishop Street
Keith House

here is Aylward Street

Portsea Secondary Modern School, Girls & Boys. Demolished in 2006.

2 The Still

First listed in 1784 as the Man and Still in the Old Rope Walk, by 1798 it had become just the Still. It retained this name or variations until closure in 1978. It was rebuilt to designs of local architect A.E.Cogswell in either 1899 or 1904 depending which reference book you believe. In 2005 the building was converted into flats, Quinnell Court.

King Street

Residential only

Kings Bench Alley

Runs from Queen Street to Kent Street

Lion Street, named after the Lion Gate which had stood separating Edinburgh Road from Queen Street from 1777 until 1871.

No properties

Lion Terrace, name derived from the nearby gate as for Lion Street.

West Side

here is Richmond Place

Richmond House, named after Richmond Place

here is Portland Street

19 R.K.Brown, Turf Accountant

24 J.Dagostino, Icecream Manufacturers

26-27 M.Gaiman & Sons Ltd., Wholesale Grocers

37 Lofty Slipper Co. Ltd., Warehouse

Little Britain Street

No Properties

North Street

East Side

19	Mrs M.Andrews, General Stores
20-21	William Trew, beer retailer
28	Bear & Staff, Alfred Bevis Listed from 1844 until 1962. The pub was demolished in January 1964.
31	Charles Parish, Greengrocer

West Side

45	F & F Hollows, Fried Fish Shop
49	Charles Taylor, Haulage Contractor, Garage
54	Red Eagle Listed in 1844 as a beer retailer, First named in 1857 as the Spread Eagle, by which name it is still known in 1887. Then until 1931 only listed as beer retailer. From 1932 until 1962 it is shown as the Red Eagle. It was demolished in 1962.

Ward House

here is King Street

Short House, demolished?

here is Cumberland Street

78-80	Duke of Edinburgh, William White Listed in 1851as a Beer Retailer at 80 North Street. In the 1863 directory is shown as The Excellents House Of Call. By 1874 it had become the Duke Of Edinburgh and from 1938 had taken in number 78. The pub closed in 1964 and after remaining derelict for some years was converted into flats being opened on 24th Mar 1988 by the Duke of Edinburgh.

Ordnance Row, named since it faced the Gunwharf.

West Side

4 Moseley & Pounsford Ltd., Outfitters
5 Goode's (Portsmouth) Ltd., Naval Tailors
6 L.G.Bendon, Café
7 Golden Sceptre
First listed in 1784 as the Golden Fleece and then with slight variations until 1905 when it is shown as the Golden Sceptre under which name it traded until 1967.
8 People's Dispensary for Sick Animals
4-8 is now the empty office block Brunel House
9-16 City Garages (Portsmouth) Ltd.

here is Victory Road
18 Gieves Ltd., Dry Cleaning Dept.
19-25 A row of fine houses, some re-fronted but the roof and rear of each gives away the age. 22 was probably earlier a shop.

here is Rosemary Lane
Linington Bros (1945) Ltd., Victory Service Station. Now demolished and forms part of the square in front of St Georges Church.

Portland Street

North Side

Jno Croad Ltd., Building Contractors, Civil Engineers, Decorators & Electrical Engineers
The business was established in 1830 by John Abraham Croad in Portland Street
here is Hay Street
A.Flemming & Co., Naval Outfitters

Prince George Street, named after the Prince George, husband of Queen Anne after whom Queen Street was named.

Not all the housing in Portsea was what would be called slums today, there were some better houses.

"76 Prince Georges Street was owned by Brickwoods and the rent was 16/–, (80p) a week. The house was enormous - four floors, basement and attic, with a wide flight of stairs at the front door and a wide entrance hall. There were lovely views from the top floor. There was a wide spiral staircase, an inside bathroom and toilet, as well as an outside toilet. That was in 1926. There was a water tap in the basement and one outside. There were chandeliers in some rooms and when it was necessary to light the gas the chandeliers had to be lowered. There was also a large back garden."

Mrs J Dyer 1975

South Side

23 F.H.Scott, Plumber
24 R.J.Goring, Scrap Metal Merchant
25 Wintworth Press Ltd., General Printers
The building was built in 1791 as a Roman Catholic Chapel, St Johns, enlarged in 1851. It was replaced by the new church in Edinburgh Road which opened as St John's Cathedral. The building was used by printers until it was demolished in 1965.
London & Southern Wholesale Co. Ltd., Grocers & Provision Merchants

North Side

30 Donald Thorne, Café
Portsea Rotary Youth Club, E.I.Jones
Rd Goring, Scrap Metal Merchant

Purbeck Street

East Side
Wemblex Shirt Co. Ltd, Shirt Manufacturers

Queen Street, named after Queen Anne whom the would be residents of Portsea petitioned to be allowed to build on Portsmouth Common.

South Side

4-5 F. Clark & Son Ltd., Naval Outfitters

here is Hay Street

8-9 C.H.Bernard & Sons Ltd., Naval outfitters

10-12 Derelict building, the Queens Cinema.
Originally a tobacco factory the building was converted into a cinema in 1914 and was still in use in 1946. Then for many years it was derelict until demolished in the 1983.

13 G.A.Cockhill & Son, Fried fish shop

14 Modiques Ltd., Silversmiths

10-12 Queen Street - Queens Theatre

16 Portsea Island Mutual Co-operative Society Ltd., Grocers
18 A. Smith, Newsagent
19 A. Smith, Hairdresser.
Earlier the Cherry Tree pub.
20 I. Daufman, Naval Tailor and Outfitter
Run by Joseph and Harold Daufman, the business was started by their father. Many years earlier was the Cock & Bottle pub.
Earlier from number 24 Queen Street was Pollards Court.

"I lived in Pollards Court in 1906. The house had three storeys, one room on each floor, a living room and two bedrooms. There was an outside pump and toilet."

Harriet Deck 1975

here is St James Street
Delaval House, named after Admiral Delaval, demolished in 2006 after being boarded up for many years. Lion House now being built by Barratt Homes on the site.
31 A. Shimbart & Son Ltd., Clothing Manufacturers
32 Red Shield House
27th Mar 1913, opened by Princess Henry of Battenberg and Hon Hedworth Meux, Commander in Chief as a Salvation Army Hostel with 100 Beds. Listed from 1923 to 1976 as Naval & Military Home, Red Shield Hostel. It was closed due to fire regulations. In Sep 1977 it re-opened as a goodwill and community centre, cost £12,000, Catherine Booth House. In 1979 the top floors converted into flats for homeless at a cost of £26,000, paid for by Dept of Environment, Salvation Army and fund raising.

here is Aylward Street
38 Mrs E.Harding, Wardrobe Dealer
Queen Street Church, Methodist Mission

The Portsea Methodists first met in Daniel Street in a chapel that was built in 1799. As the brewery gradually bought up all the premises in the area the chapel ended up in the middle of the large

Queen Street Wesleyan

brewery complex. On the 16th December 1912 the tender of Messrs Evans for £2,882 for a new chapel in Queen Street was accepted. The architect was local man Edwin Smith. £55 was paid to Brunswick for premises on site. On 5th March 1913 the foundation stones were laid by Mrs R.H.Tamsett, Mr Parham, Mr Kimber, Mr Watkins and Mr Curtiss. The church was opened on 20th August 1913. In February 1949 it was reported that building was scheduled category 1 under the Town and Country planning act - likely to be requisitioned and demolished. Despite this the building was still in use in 1965 but was in a very bad state as little money had been spent due to the scheduling. At this point it was found that the repairs required were beyond the means of the congregation and in 1968 the building was purchased by the Corporation for £5,250 and demolished. The site is now a open green space.

here is Bishop Street

44 Salvation Army Goodwill Centre

Opened in 1916 as a Slum Post, on 14th September 1942 it was registered for worship, de-registered in 1977. Latterly it was the Salvation Army Goodwill Centre.

The shops and houses in this stretch of the street show what the whole of the street would have been like in earlier days. Not uniform terraces but each plot developed with a mixture of plain two storey houses and grand three or four storey houses.

45 Mrs Nathan Salome, Bookseller
46 Service Café, Albert Aycliffe
47 N.J.Harrison, Grocer
48 Jack Blair, L.George proprietor, Naval Tailor & Outfitters
49 W.Cooper(Harwich) Ltd., Naval Outfitters

here are King's Bench Alley and Curzon Howe Road

57-58 J.O.Foster Ltd., Butchers
59 Harkin Ltd., Tobacconists
60 Allen Searle, Hairdressers
61 Campions (Bakers) Ltd.

here is Southampton Row

63 Bert Osborne, Cycle Dealer

Carter House, not named after the Carter family, brewers and local politicians, but like the other Portsea flats after an Admiral.

here is Hanover Street

Portsmouth Royal Sailors Home Club, Lt-Cmdr W.Miller, RN, retd

81-82 J.Baker & Co Ltd., Naval Outfitters

here is Hawke Street

84 The King George

Became a pub in 1782, named the George in 1784. Has traded as George and variations to date. Has the only surviving example of Jewell & Sons in ceramic faced tiles on the facade. They were the predecessors to Brickwoods at Portsea.

85 Waltons Surgical Appliance Co, Surgical appliance manufacturers

Now part of the extended King George.

Drake House, named after the Admiral.

here is Havant Street

Camden Known as the Hat in Hand from 1784 until 1905. Rebuilt in 1904 to designs of local architect A.E.Cogswell. Listed as the Camden from 1911 until 1976 when it was converted into a Naval Community facility as part of the Royal Sailors Rest organisation. Opened by Lady Williams wife of the then Second Sea Lord on 28th July 1976.

North Side

104a Fryer's Laundry Ltd

104a British Sailors Society, Café

here are Admiralty Road, Daniel Street and Cross Streets

122 George Donaldson, Chemist

123 Greenburgh Bros. Ltd., Outfitters

125 London & Southern Wholesale Co. Ltd., Wholesale Grocers & Provision Merchants

Queen Street

126	Greenburgh Bros. Ltd., Naval Outfitters
127	Mrs L.Bevis, Wool Shop
128	H.Gattenberg, Greengrocers
129	Bertie Greentree, Tobacconist
130	Chapman's Laundry, Receiving Office
135	J.W.Tout, Marine & General Engineer
136	Myer Geller, Boot Repairer
137	Clothing Productions Ltd., Wholesale Clothing Manufacturers
138	C.M.Smitherman, Wardrobe Dealer
139	Frederick Laver, Boot Repairer
140	Harbour Motorcyles (A.W.Baker, proprietor), Specialists in repairs, overhauls and tuning
141	Harris & Son, Funeral Directors
142	Curzon Howe, Mrs M.Ward

	Was earlier an off licence. It lasted until 1965 when it was demolished.
144	Mrs A Harding, Wardrobe Dealer
145	John Conway Ltd., Naval Outfitters
146	Charles Kemp & Son, General Ironmongers, Glass & China Specialists
151	Potts & Horsey, Printers
153	H.Segal Ltd., Outfitters
154-155	Holbrook & Son Ltd., Printers
	Started in 1850 when Arthur Holbrook bought the Portsmouth Times newspaper printing company that been founded in 1802. The company are still in operation in Norway Road.
158	Mrs A Morris, Watchmakers
159-160	The Bargain Shop, Antique Dealers

here is North Street

168	Mrs M.Deakin, Wardrobe Dealer
169	Unifit, Naval Outfitters
170	Jack Helman, Shopkeeper

here is York Place

171	Royal Oak Hotel
	Dates back to at least 1784, possibly 1716. It was demolished in 1966.
172	Baun & Co., Naval Outfitters
174	Erlich & Son Ltd., Naval Outfitters
175	Pearkes Dairies Ltd., Grocers
177	L.Zeffertt & Sons Ltd., Tailors
179	Fran's, Ladies' Hairdresser
182	Baun & Co., Naval Outfitters
184	Field (Cleaners) Ltd., Dyers & Cleaners
186	Acme Printing Co. Ltd., Printers
188	Fleet Outfitting Stores, Naval Outfitters
189	Jerome Goss Co., Tobacconists
	In 1856 James Collis established his wholesale tobacconists business here.

190 Queen Street

190 Royal Standard

Listed in 1823 as Sir John Barleycorn which name was used until 1847. Then in the 1851 directory it is the Royal Standard which it remained until 1972 when it was demolished. The view below is from a glass negative retrieved from a skip by one of our members.

191 Royal Naval Arms

Listed from1798 until 1901 as the Kings Arms, and from 1899 to 1971 when it was demolished as the Royal Naval Arms. The two year overlap is probably a directory mistake as the pub was rebuilt in 1899 to designs of local architect A.E.Cogswell and was probably renamed at that time. Some references have it listed as being rebuilt in 1916 but that is possibly an error.

here is Military Row
Richmond Place

South Side

St George's Primary School, Junior Mixed

"I was Portsmouth born and bred and I wanted a teaching job. I had an interview at the Education Office in the Easter and then towards the end of the final term I had a letter from the Headmaster of the school, and I looked at the heading on the note-paper and it said St George's School, Portsea. That was in July 1954 and I started at the school in September and never regretted it. It was rather amusing to find my way there really, because I had no idea where it was. A friend of mine offered to take me down and see if we could find it. We came down one evening about a week or two before the summer holiday ended, we knew it was off Lion Terrace somewhere and came down onto Richmond Place and there was this building. There was no notice to say it was St George's School, but carved in stone over the windows it said 'Portsea Ragged School'. There was a public house next door and somebody was leaning in the doorway smoking a cigarette; so we asked this gentleman if the school was called St George's School, because on the window of the public house it said St George's Tap. He said 'I don't know the name of the school at all'. But we gathered that it was the right school and on the first day of term when I turned up it happened to be the right one. The Headmaster, Mr N.J.Collings, was conscious of the fact that there was no board outside so he had one made.

It wasn't a very impressive looking building and the Headmaster apologised to me for starting my teaching career there. I said ' Well it's not the building, it's the people that make the school'. We had five classrooms. Downstairs, there were two rooms divided by a sliding partition and every morning the whole school assembled there. The partition was pushed back and we stood around the

Richmond Place School

walls. Those that were in the two classes of course remained in their seats. When I joined, the school was beginning to burst at the seams, and they already had a class away from the building which was on the other side of Queen Street in Prince George Street. It was the old church hall of St John's Church. The church had been bombed in the war but the hall escaped. Anyway the hall was where the Rotary Club met and it was also used as a Youth Club in the evening. I had to go over there as a new teacher with a class, so the year I started we had two classes in the same hall. We could each hear the other teacher teaching and in between there was a canvas screen on wheels. The desks and chairs were put out by the caretaker and one of the perks we had was he used to have a lovely cup of tea waiting for us in the morning. The children came up from the Beneficial School at seven. The teacher next door had the seven year olds and I taught the eight year olds.

In 1960 the new St George's School was built so I spent six years in the old buildings. One of the governors of the school was a director at Brickwoods and he asked the headmaster if he could use the old pub. So the upstairs rooms became the Headmaster and secretaries offices and the old bar was turned into the school library"

Mr Spencer 1982

St George's Square, named after the church. New flats were being built in 1957 to accommodate residents affected by the slum clearance programme. Walter Besant the novelist was born at number 3 in 1836. In the seventies the square was spilt in two with the 'northern' part becoming St Georges Way.

South-East Side

here is Richmond Place
St George's House
Freemantle House, named after Admiral Freemantle, demolished by 2004.

here is Britain Street
From the mid sixties until the mid seventies Crockerills Ltd, clothing manufacturers were here re-locating from several previous addresses. Although they did make women's underwear, readers will probably best remember them

for their childrens' range under the name Ladybird.

North-West Side

2	A grey brick house of unusual shape built around 1760
4	A render fronted merchants house dating from 1796
38	Campions (Bakers) Ltd., Registered Offices, Bakeries & Despatch Garage Founded in 1779 by William Miller a close friend of William Vosper

Raleigh House, named after the Admiral.
Grenville House, named after the Admiral.
St Georges Clinic, City of Portsmouth Education Committee, Clinic & Child Welfare

88	A very smart stucco faced three storey building shows how much of the square may have looked in earlier days. Originally it would have been one house.
94-96	Eagle Tavern First listed in 1784 as The Blue Anchor, the name it kept until 1851. The pub was rebuilt in 1853 and in 1859 is shown as the Eagle, variations of which were used until 1976. In 1988 after laying derelict it was converted into flats.

here is Butcher Street
St George's Church

In 1752 an Act of Parliament for building of a church was passed. The site was given by the Corporation for a yearly rent one peppercorn. On the 11th May 1753 the foundation stones were laid by Richard Poate, William Maine, Thomas Gill, Richard Coles and John Loney. The architect was Nicholas Vass and the cost was £2,208 9s with seats for 979.

The money raised from sale of seats priced from £5 to £36, raised £1,979. On 17th September 1754 the church was consecrated by the Bishop of Chichester. The church was renovated from 1949 to 1951 at a cost of £12,000 paid for by the War Department. In 2001 another refurbishment at a cost of £180,000 was carried out.

St James Street

East Side

1-3	I.Daufman, Tailor
4	Ronald Gisborne, Seed Merchant

here is Beck Street

9	Portsdown Ice Cream Co., Ice Cream Manufacturers
9	W.G.Wilson & Sons, Builders

here is Lion Street

10	Three Crowns Inn First listed in 1798, the pub has traded under variations of the name until the present day.
13-14	Portsmouth Wiping Cloth Co., Rag Merchants

West Side

School Clinic, Portsmouth Education Committee

37	Charles Stanley Taylor & Son Ltd., Haulage & Removal Contractors
38	Norman Vick, Shopkeeper

Southampton Row

Runs from Queen Street to Kent Street.

Union Street, named after the Union of Scotland and England. In 1957 new flats were being built to accommodate the families affected by the slum clearance programme.

East Side

37-38	G.H.Kirby, Greengrocer

Victory Road was Ankersmiths Lane, then Smiths Lane. In 1896 the old houses were pulled down and in 1898 the developer requested that the name be changed to Victory Road.
Wickham Street, some properties were demolished in the 1957 slum clearance programme.

East Side

1	Norrey & Sons, Grocers
6	Old Free House Listed as beer retailer in 1874 then named in 1881 as the Old Free House. In 1983 the two bar pub was renovated and re-opened as The Invincible.

York Place

Residential Only

"I lived with the Peronne family at 20 York Place from 1928 to 1930. The house was then left empty because it was due for demolition under a slum clearance scheme. The Peronne family were musicians. The house consisted of basement, ground floor (two rooms and a scullery), first floor (one large room, one smaller room) and two attic rooms. I paid 5/- (25p) for my first floor room. The Peronne family also made ice-cream in the scullery and sold hot chestnuts in the winter. The condition of the house was good structurally, but terribly neglected, plaster and wallpaper coming away from the walls. There was an inside water tap and a flush lavatory at the end of the garden."

Mr Philip Puntis 1975

As part of the revision of this booklet it was decided to add the Gunwharf Quays which are now, after a few hundred years of various Government uses, open as a new public area. To fully explain the area we include the development of the area from the early days through to the redevelopment.

Starting with the early history.

The building of the Old Gun Wharf commenced in 1662. The contractor for its construction was William Shakespeare (not the playwright between plays, but a contractor from London), and immense excavations between the areas of Portsea which became Hanover Street, Union Street, Kent Street and Queen Street, were formed by the removal of soil (by permission of the Corporation) for the purpose of raising the shore and reclaiming land from the sea. The first storehouses were built in 1669 and the officers houses in 1719.

HMS Vernon Office Building

Under the Duke of Richmond, Master General of Ordnance, the establishment was much enlarged and improved. A new armoury was built in 1797 for 21,000 stands of arms. The New Gun Wharf was commenced in 1797 on suggestion of General Bentham, designed by General Evelegh.

The soil came from the new basin being dug out in the Dockyard. The boundary wall was built in 1803 and there were two gates, the piers of one gate surmounted by stone mortars. (This gate is still in situ and once more visible to the public, near the Vulcan building.) Around 1800/1810 a small storehouse was built which by 1836 it had become The Royal Marines Infirmary, later just known as The Infirmary. On 28th Nov 1811 the Duke of Clarence laid the

Gunwharf Armoury

HM Gunwharf from sea

foundation stone for a new storehouse that consisted of three sides of a square, in its centre is a large archway surmounted by a clock. (This was later known as No 21 building or the Vulcan building.) On the same wharf was erected a Small Sea Armoury and magazine. Meanwhile on the old gunwharf a new office block was built in 1810.

In 1891 the gunwharf was split in two with the Navy being given all the stores on one side of the creek, the Army the stores on the other side of the creek. At the same time the gunwharf was extended and new wall built which survives as the current boundary wall.

The armoury was open to the public and contained splendid examples of the armour and weapons used from the time of Cressy and Agincourt. This collection formed the basis of the displays at the Tower of London and later Leeds.

Based on material from Gates History of Portsmouth, who borrowed much of the material from an earlier work by Henry Slight, with additions from HGP Greentree Allchurch Evans Ltd.

Development in the twentieth century.

HMS Vernon which most people will connect with the gunwharf was originally a group of old wooden walled hulks in the harbour, one of which was HMS Vernon. The 'ship' moved ashore in October 1923, there were apart from the instructional side, three departments' Whitehead, Mining and Electrical. Some new blocks were built to suit the new use. In 1935 one of the old blocks, built as barracks, caught fire and was half burnt out.

In the Second World War there were several air raids that involved the establishment. In the 24th August 1940 raid, the Alexandra Training Building was hit, some of the staff were then moved to Leigh Park House and West Leigh House at Havant. Other staff went to Portsmouth Grammar School, but following incendiary damage to that they moved to the Rechabite Hall, London Road. Another department evacuated to Clarence Pier. Another raid on 5th December 1940 damaged the remaining part of the Alexandra Building. The Wardroom silver had been removed to Curtiss' Repository which was destroyed in the 10th Jan 1941 raid when the repository was hit. As well as large areas of Portsmouth the remaining part of Building 17 and the Clock Tower of building 21 were destroyed by incendiary bombs. Clarence Pier was also bombed and the staff had to relocate to the Alberta Hotel and the Royal Albert Yacht Club. In the raids of the 9-10 March 1941 the Mining Tank (The large building that dominated the skyline of HMS Vernon) and the Princess Margaret Building were damaged. The following day another raid destroyed the Dido Building. The final incendiary raid on HMS Vernon was on the night of the 27-28th April 1941.

Reconstruction started in 1945 with the North and West Blocks on the south side of the creek and a new officers block on the north side. Donegal House was to be demolished as was the north wing of the Vulcan Block, building 21. In 1956 the Mohawk Block was demolished to make way for a new Petty Officers' accommodation block. From 1953 up to 100 pigs were kept in a Danish style piggery with at first 15 a month being used for internal consumption, later 100 a quarter were sent to the Fatstock Marketing Board. Ducks and geese were kept on the pond but these appear to be for ornamental purposes only.

HMS Vernon 1930-1955. Commander E.Webb

Road names of HMS Vernon, Acteon Road, Ariadne Road, Captain's Walk, Defiance Road, Dolphin Way, Fisher Road, Main Road, Scott Road and Vulcan Road.

Latest redevelopment to form Gunwharf Quays.

In 1998 re-development of the site was commenced by Berkeley Group and Lordland C.C. It was to be developed as a mixture of mostly commercial property and public space on the northern, old gunwharf, with mostly private housing on the old southern, Gunwharf. The underground car park is reputedly the largest in the world and involved excavating out a lot of the soil that had a few hundred years earlier been used in reclamation. A few of the old buildings were preserved.

The infirmary of 1800/1810 was converted into six apartments. Later in 2000 also under direction of architects HGP Greentree Allchurch Evans Ltd, the south wing and centre block of the Vulcan building of 1811 were restored by Walter Llewellyn and Sons Ltd . This included the replacement of the clock and clock tower and rebuilding the north wing entirely. While the restoration was in hand large tanks were found underground, those under the north and south wings are thought to have been rainwater tanks. In the tank under the central block thousands of flints shaped for flint lock guns were found. Other buildings retained include: the Bridge Keeper's Cottage of 1800 now mistakenly called the Lock-keepers cottage; the Police House of 1877 by the main gate; the shell store of 1856 with four feet thick walls still stands alongside the Vulcan building; the Vernon Office Building has been converted into The Old Customshouse, public house.

New road names: Caen Marche, Central Square, Marlborough Avenue, Mercator Avenue, New Hampshire Boulevard, Philip Avenue, Sirius Avenue, Togo Avenue, Vernon Avenue and The Waterfront.

New housing names: Anson Court, Arethusa House, Blake House, The Blue Building, Brecon House, Canalside, The Crescent, Jupiter Court, Lighthouse, Number 1, Lysander Court, Minerva Crescent and the Old Infirmary.

Memories of HMS Vernon.

"As a small child I often heard my Dad tell of the time he spent working in HMS Vernon, during the First World War in the sea mines department and how on one occasion he was one of a group that took a German sea mine by rail to London. So from those tales he told, I generated an interest in HMS Vernon - this ancient and important part of the sea defences of our country. For those of us of the younger generation it always had an air of adventure and mystery about it with its armed sentries at its gates!

During the 1939-1945 war once again HMS Vernon undertook a major part in the vicious sea war that threatened the Nation's existence - the Dunkirk evacuation, Dieppe and afterwards many of the expeditions to harass the French coastline.

I married my wife Phyllis in 1946 and in the late 1960s we took our took our two children to the tattoos which were held in the grounds of the Vernon. It was a treat to be able to visit the spacious grounds of this establishment which hitherto had been closed to the public and view the buildings, workshops and maintenance facilities available. The event took place in the evening with a variety of events making up the event from all sections of the armed forces. Motor cycle displays from the Army, RAF with their police dogs showing how they were used to apprehend intruders on airfields finishing with the most thrilling tricks, and finally jumping through hoops of fire. The Navy gave a demonstration of climbing and manning the huge portable mainmast they had erected, finishing with a presentation to the seaman who ended as Button Boy standing on the very top of the mast.

There was one event that thrilled the audience - the demonstration by the Parachute Regiment where they jumped from their plane and landed on an illuminated circle on the parade ground. Unfortunately on the last occasion we attended one of the parachutists landed on an iron spiked fence and had to be taken to hospital. A sad incident.

The Royal Marines gave their usual immaculate display of marching and counter marching to their magnificent bands with their Corp of Drums and Bugles finishing the evening playing the traditional Last Post. Before we left Vernon, people would stand and watch the officers and their wives leave the pavilion where they had been seated and walk to the Officers Mess, in order to admire the splendour of their uniforms and the dresses of the ladies.

Alas the Vernon is now replaced by Gunwharfs Quays - a conglomeration of factory outlet shops, ugly huge blocks of flats totally divorced from the beautiful open space it always has been with views of the harbour spoilt. If you look at what's being built now you could not be blamed if you believed the Council and the architects were mad and sadly have let the citizens of the City down."

Frank Deacon.

"After completing a regular period of service with the Royal Engineers, I was employed in the works department with the Admiralty situated in the Naval

Establishment of HMS Vernon. It was early in 1957 and because of this the area which not only included the harbour, main railway station, but the main gate of the Dockyard and there was always a great deal of activity.

Although the history of this naval shore base dates back to when it was known as the Gunwharf being mostly concerned with the shipment of arms. It was now a very important and active naval shore base. During this period in time this base consisting of instruction areas, administration blocks, a sports complex and large accommodation blocks housing probably two thousand officers and ratings. Security of course was very strict and both gates were continually manned by naval guards.

The obvious responsibility of the works department was to maintain the whole area regarding building and services. Civilian staff for this purpose probably included two hundred personnel including all the recognised trades. I enjoyed working in this place as the atmosphere among the working staff was always very good and a helping hand was always available. However, during the last few weeks of employment I was detailed to inspect a certain area of fencing surrounding the United Services Sports Ground. On examination I discovered a small section of rail needing bolting together. I realised that including travelling time to and from the Vernon the job could be completed in just a few hours. I reported back to the office and was told to complete the necessary work for security reasons. It so happened that at this time it was the beginning of the cricket season and Yorkshire County Cricket Club were due to play in the county championship against Hampshire. As the match was a three day game strange as it may seem the job concerning the repair of the railings also lasted for three days!!

A month or two after this happy final period of employment I completed my time in the Vernon but it will always be a happy memory to have worked in this interesting area.

Later when my daughter, Diane, was a pupil at the Southern Grammar School for Girls she became friendly with a girl in her class who had a great interest in music. Both girls were highly graded both with piano and oboe and Diane often would be invited to her friend's home to practice with her music loving parents, Mr and Mrs Taylor.

There were times when due to Mr Taylor's connections with the Navy they would be invited to the music hall in the Vernon to practice in a wind quintet, one of the other players being a serving member of the Officers' Mess. However, on one particular Friday evening a very important person happened to be in the city on a business and during the evening paid a visit to the Officers' Mess. This person although an accomplished musician did not play a instrument but stayed a while to listen and enjoy the musical practice. After light refreshments with the officers and players he departed. The VIP was in fact Mr Edward Heath."

Don Tallack

Finally returning in time a former resident William Tarring wrote memories of several areas of Portsmouth, in the 1840s to 60s, and those on Portsea follow:

"Leaving Portsmouth by the aforesaid arch and passing over the accommodation bridge and pathway through the earthworks we emerged with the Kings Mill on the left and the Mill Dam on the right, then passing the outer fortifications of military bridge over the Mill race, we came to the town proper with the Gunwharf gates on the west side, on the other side was the Public House, Elephant & Castle *[St. Georges Square]* and Rannies Iron Foundry all since swept away. At the back of St.Georges Church the hustings were erected I think in 1865 when W.H.Stone and Serjeant Gaselee were elected. Many years previously there had been an important waxwork exhibition in the square the leading item being Androcles and the Lion with moving effects. The show broke up and the band were left derelict.

The gas offices used to be at the upper end and opposite to it on the spur was a very tall special lamppost which was moved to a position opposite the Clarence Esplanade Pier. The house at the corner now a part of Totterdell's Hotel was the residence of Dr.E.J.Scott who operated on my eye. When I was quite a little child, I ran a pair of scissors in my eye which caused great trouble. My memory is so vivid because it was before the time of anaesthetics, and I had to bear the pain. My Grandmother with Spartan firmness held me in the chair while Scott assisted by Mr.Parsons who was in partnership and afterwards succeeded to the business and continued to be our family doctor until about 1880.

The Portsea Police Station was in the rear of the Hotel and I have a vague recollection of the Stocks which stood there. At any rate I remember the fuss there was about the last man who occupied them. Scotts surgery stood at the corner, about the first house in Ordnance Row. The dispenser (Bigwood) had a hair lip and was an eccentric character. He afterwards opened a chemist's shop in St.James Street where he was the sport of rude boys. He afterwards had a chemist shop in Church Road, Kingston and looked after the Post Office there.

One day a friend stopped him to enquire after Mrs.Bigwood when he was informed that "Martha had misbehaved herself and he had locked her up in her bedroom".

The Hampshire Library was an important object, but like other literary objects in Portsmouth it came to grief and to the disgrace it was sold and went out of the Town. Portsmouth was never celebrated for its literary excellence. The Portsmouth Philosophical Society gave way to a Masonic Lodge. The Athenaeum in Portsea and the Watt Institute at Landport, both died a lingering death a specimen of Portsmouth intelligence appeared in the Portsmouth Times in a report of a Council meeting Alderman Moses Solomon opposed the introduction of the "Health of Towns Act". In the course of his remarks he said "T'wasn't the bad smells that made people ill it was the damp moisture of the atmospherey weather, got into people's insides and couldn't be digested." Solomons kept a curiosity shop in Ordnance Row and had a branch in Pier Street, Ryde, I.O.W. Next door to him lived retired Commander Kye with a rather eccentric record there was also a printer named Woodward and Atkins a music seller, who built St. Georges Hall and Mr. Henry Emanuel a useful member of the Town Council. Next, the Common Hard end, was the residence of Mr. Ezekial Emanuel which after his death was converted into a music and dancing saloon and nighthouse under the name of "The Wheatsheaf". It gained for itself a very bad reputation, I forebear from mentioning what. I heard of its doings through a member of the band.

Common Hard commenced after passing the Gunwharf and the first item to attract attention was the main drain of the Portsea System which flowed into the Harbour at low tide. I remember W.H.Woodin a popular entertainer of the day at St. Georges Hall introduced a topical verse into a singsong he was singing. He sang that it seemed as if the Inspector of Nuisances had lost his nose and "didn't know where to find it".

1847 again I remember the rejoicings at the opening of the "Royal Albert Pier". It was never a grand success and was swept away when the Railway was constructed. There was nothing very noticeable about the houses on the Hard most of which were licensed houses. Towards the Dockyard gates there were a few shops one of which was run by Crassweller who was Chairman of the Portsea Commissioners, and who took a great interest in the maintenance of the cleanliness of the streets and was quite an extra and unpaid inspector of nuisance. It did credit to his care. He was a dealer in crockery ware. Chambers the grocer was always there.

For many years there was a kind of market held on the pavement by the people from Portchester which was discontinued when the market in Commercial Road got more important.

The Dockyard gate here reminds me of my golden number again, in 1847 I saw the only double launch held in Portsmouth Dockyard. The Arrogant and the Plumper were built on adjacent slips and were launched on the same tide in my presence. I saw a number of launches at different times but the most notable was that of the Marlborough. A great fuss was made over it, because Queen Victoria performed the christening, after she did so instead of cutting the cord to let the dog shores fall, she was conducted in great state to a pavilion at the stern specially erected for her to witness the ship take to the water. The delay was dangerous for the tide had turned, and the stern swung round and the ship refused to move, it was a time of danger and the Queen soon made herself scarce. It was a most anxious time for the shipwright authorities but the launch was successfully accomplished on the next tide. By a singular co-incidence, the Duchess of Marlborough, a collier hung up the next day at Byerley's Yard, Rudmore.

In 1848 I was present at the opening of the Steam Basin by the Queen, I was on the roof of one of the buildings and saw the tiny yacht Elfin steam into the basin followed by a fleet of small boats. The Queen landed on the east side and accompanied by the old Duke of Wellington walked partly round the basin. When she reached the south side, just beneath our position, one the pattern makers, who happened to possess a Cornet, gave vent to his loyalty by blaring out the National Anthem, an item not on the programme. I was entered on the lists and stopped of school into work on the 11th of February 1854.

I could write of a number of things connected with Portsea but must be content with one item viz, the riot between the 50th Duke of Wellington's Regiment and the crew of one of the ships in the harbour. It commenced in a brothel in Whites Row and assumed threatening proportions. The Mayor read the Riot Act in Queen Street and Lord FitzClarence who was Lieut Governor at the time took a firm stand with the military. The sailors were kept on board their ship and the soldiers confined to Barracks but they broke out and paraded their vengeance. I saw them streaming up the Commercial Road in two's and three's, and one of them turned into Thomas Street and pulled a tuft of grass where with to wipe the blood off the buckle of his belt. At one time the sailors had assembled in full force in Whites Row and the Boatswains mate had piped "All hands down house" the rope was actually affixed to a chimney stack for that purpose when news was brought to them that a poor girl was lying in an upstairs room dying. This fact saved the situation.

In this connection there was one more "Lord Bacon" incident. Pickets had been parading the streets for the purpose of picking up any stray dis-orderlies. A marine who as hurrying down to catch his boat was intercepted. Bacon happening to come along at the time took in the situation at a glance. Putting on his best naval officers air, he crossed over and harangued the man "What does this mean Johnson? Didn't I tell you to be down at the boat by seven o'clock. I'll make you smart for this. Serjeant I'll see to this man. Follow me sir". He then walked off in his grandest style followed by the man in wonderment. As soon as they had got round the corner out of sight "Bacon" said to him "Run y'fool for your life." Tableaux! One more incident and I have done. At one time there was a heavy downpour of rain and a number of people had sought shelter in the small arch at Lion Gate "Bacon" came along in full Mackintosh rig. Something in his appearance raised a laugh, turning sharply around he said "What are you laughing at? If you are not careful I'll have you turned out of this." This speech caused more laughter. "Sentry" he called "call the serjeant of the Guard" Serjeant of the Guard turn out on his appearance "Bacon" said "Serjeant I'm an officer of the so and so and have been grossly insulted in this arch, order your men out and turn them out." "Guard turn out" and out bundled about a dozen soldiers with their muskets in hand and the eviction took place everyone being turned out in the pouring rain. Tableaux! Adieu "Bacon"

The old surroundings of the Town had a beauty all of their own, the ramparts with their fine elm trees , the winding roads with their flanking ramparts made a very pleasant walk. Near the top was Five Posts Lane a short route to Pinks stile, this was an accommodation path cut by the authorities through the Ravelin to accommodate foot passengers and when Alfred Road was made in its stead, it was made winding in order to try and save some fine elm trees but in vain. The new road so under cut the level of the roots that the trees soon died.